Schöningh

Discover ...

SHAKESPEARE TEXTS
edited by Engelbert Thaler

William Shakespeare
The Sonnets

by Anke Weber

Sprachliche Betreuung: Simone Duxbury-Ziemer

www.schoeningh-schulbuch.de
Schöningh Verlag, Jühenplatz 1–3, 33098 Paderborn

Druck 5 4 3 2 1 / Jahr 2014 13 12 11 10
Die letzte Zahl bezeichnet das Jahr dieses Druckes.

Umschlaggestaltung: Franz-Josef Domke, Hannover
Umschlagabbildung: © vario images
Druck und Bindung: westermann druck GmbH, Braunschweig

ISBN 978-3-14-040114-2

Contents

Getting started

- Complete the following sentence: 'Love is ...'
- On the right, you see three people who lived around 1600. Imagine the three of them were sitting in a room together. What might they be thinking about love? Write a short statement for each of them.
- Compare your answers and make a list of the various facets of love you have come up with.

- Shakespeare's 154 sonnets mainly deal with love. Before taking a closer look at them and finding out more about his view of love, you might try to write your own poem on love. You can choose any form you like and can concentrate on the aspect of love you find most interesting.

Love is ...
Love is ...
Love is ...

'Shall I Compare Thee to ...' – Interpretation of Poetry

Wooing Women – Shakespeare in 'Dead Poets Society'

Tom Schulman

Peter Weir's movie 'Dead Poets Society' (1989) is set in 1959 at the conservative U.S. prep school Welton Academy, which is an all-boys school. It depicts the story of a new English teacher, Mr John Keating, who manages to inspire his students with his love and enthusiasm for language and literature. The following texts are extracts from the screenplay. Knox Overstreet, Todd Anderson, Neil Perry and Charlie Dalton are some of Mr Keating's students, who are confronted with his somewhat unorthodox teaching methods. He has just made them tear out a chapter on measuring a poem's perfection by J. Evans Pritchard, which he believes to be nonsense.

Chemistry lesson

KEATING: Keep ripping, gentlemen. This is a battle, a war. And the casualties could be your hearts and souls. Thank you, Mr Dalton. – Armies of academics going forward measuring poetry. No! We'll not have that here! No more Mr J. Evans Pritchard! Now, my class, you'll learn to think for yourselves again. You will learn to savour words and language. No matter what anybody tells you, words and ideas can change the world. Now, I see that look in Mr Pitt's eye, like 19th century literature has nothing to do with going to business school or medical school. Right? Maybe. Mr Hopkins, you may agree with him, thinking: "Yes, we should simply study our Mr Pritchard and learn to read our rhyme and metre and go quietly about the business of achieving other ambitions." I have a secret for you. Huddle up. Huddle up! (*The students move closer to him.*)

Do you think it is justified that all ► children are made to read "old" literature at school, no matter what they want to do with their lives?

to huddle up to come nearer, crouching

Mr Keating's English lesson

We don't read and write poetry because it's cute. We read and write poetry because we are members of the human race and the human race is filled with passion. And medicine, business, law, engineering, these are noble pursuits and necessary to sustain life. But poetry, beauty, romance, love, these are what we stay alive for. To quote from Whitman: "O me! O life! of the questions of these recurring, Of the endless trains of the faithless, of cities filled with the foolish. What good amid these, O me, O life?" Answer: That you are here. That life exists, and identity. That the powerful play goes on, and you may contribute a verse. (*with more emphasis*) That the powerful play goes on, and you may contribute a verse." What will your verse be?

Whitman Walter Whitman (1819–1892), American poet and journalist
recurring something that keeps on coming back

◀ In which way do you want to contribute? 'What will your verse be?'

The next day, Mr Keating teaches his class more about the power of language, and Shakespeare's language in particular.

KEATING: A man is not very tired. He is exhausted! And don't use, "very sad" Use – Come on, Mr Overstreet, you twerp.

twerp (*colloq.*) silly boy

KNOX OVERSTREET: Morose?

KEATING: Exactly! Morose. – Now, language was developed for one endeavour and that is? Mr Anderson?

TODD ANDERSON: (*does not reply*)

KEATING: Come on! Are you a man or an amoeba? (*laughter*) – Mr Perry?

amoeba a unicellular being

NEIL PERRY: Uh, to communicate.

KEATING: No. To woo women. (*laughter*) Today we're going to be talking about William Shakespeare.

STUDENTS: Oh, God!

KEATING: I know. A lot of you look forward to this about as much as you look forward to root canal work. We are gonna talk about Shakespeare as someone who writes something

root canal work painful dental treatment

very interesting. Now many of you have seen Shakespeare done very much like this: (*speaks through his nose*) "Oh Titus, bring your friend hither!" But if any of you have seen Mr Marlon Brando (*imitates Brando*) you know that Shakespeare can be different: "Friends, Romans, countrymen, lend me your ears." (*laughter*) You can also imagine maybe John Wayne as Macbeth going (*imitates John Wayne*) "Well, is this a dagger I see before me?" (*laughter*)

Encouraged by Mr Keating, the students found the 'Dead Poets Society', a secret club that meets at night-time in a cave in the forest to read, to act and to savour poetry. Gradually, these meetings also begin to influence the students' everyday lives. One night, Charlie Dalton surprises his classmates by asking two girls to join the club.

STEVEN MEEKS: Oh, my God!

GIRL'S VOICE: Is this it?

CHARLIE DALTON: Yeah, this is it. Go ahead, go in! It's my cave. Watch your step.

GIRL'S VOICE: We're not gonna slip, are we? Uh-oh. (*to the other boys*) Hi.

GERALD PITTS: (*gets up and hits his head at the ceiling*) Hello.

OTHERS: Hello.

CHARLIE: Hi guys. Meet, uh, Gloria and ehm –

TINA: Tina.

CHARLIE: Tina. This is the pledge class of the Dead Poets Society.

EVERYONE: Hello. How do you do? Hello. Hi. Hi.

CHARLIE: Guys, move, move! Come on folks. It's Friday night. Let's get on with the meeting.

OTHERS: (*move*) Sorry. Excuse me, excuse me.

Charlie woos Tina

Charlie wins Gloria over

CHARLIE: Guys, I have an announcement to make. In keeping with this spirit of passionate experimentation of the Dead Poets, I am giving up the name Charles Dalton. From now on, call me Nuwanda.

OTHERS: Nuwanda? (*laugh*)

(*Charlie takes Tina's lipstick and draws some stripes on his face*)

(*a little later*)

CHARLIE: (*sits down*) Are we gonna have a meeting or what?

GLORIA: Yeah. If you guys don't have a meeting, how do we know if you want to join?

NEIL: (*astonished*) Join?

CHARLIE: (*to Tina*) "Shall I compare thee to a summer's day? Thou art more lovely and more temperate."

◀ Beginning of Shakespeare's Sonnet No. 18

TINA: That's so sweet.

CHARLIE: I made that up. Just for you.

TINA: You did?

CHARLIE: I'll write one for you too, Gloria. (*turns to her*) "She walks in beauty like the night – She walks in beauty like the night. Of cloudless climes and starry skies. All that's best, dark and bright meet in her aspect and her eyes."

◀ Beginning of a poem by George Byron (1788–1824), 6th Baron Byron, English romanticist poet

GLORIA: That's beautiful.

CHARLIE: There's plenty more where that came from.

Activities

The meaning of poetry

1. Explain Mr Keating's view of poetry. Do you agree?
2. 'No matter what anybody tells you, words and ideas can change the world.' – Find examples to support Mr Keating's view.

Experimenting with poetry

3. a) Try to find an English poem that means a lot to you personally. If you do not know any English poems or do not have a collection of English poems at home, the following homepage might help: www.poemhunter.com/poems
   b) Present this poem to the class and explain why you have chosen this particular poem.

4. Below you will find the complete Sonnet No. 18 by William Shakespeare. Experiment with it: Try to recite it in an interesting and meaningful way.

Express yourself

5. 'A man is not very tired. He is exhausted!' – Find as many better expressions as possible for the following commonly overused words: good, bad, sad, happy, nice, hungry, friendly, unfriendly, beautiful, ugly, hot, cold, intelligent, stupid.

Sonnet No. 18 – "Shall I Compare Thee to a Summer's Day?"

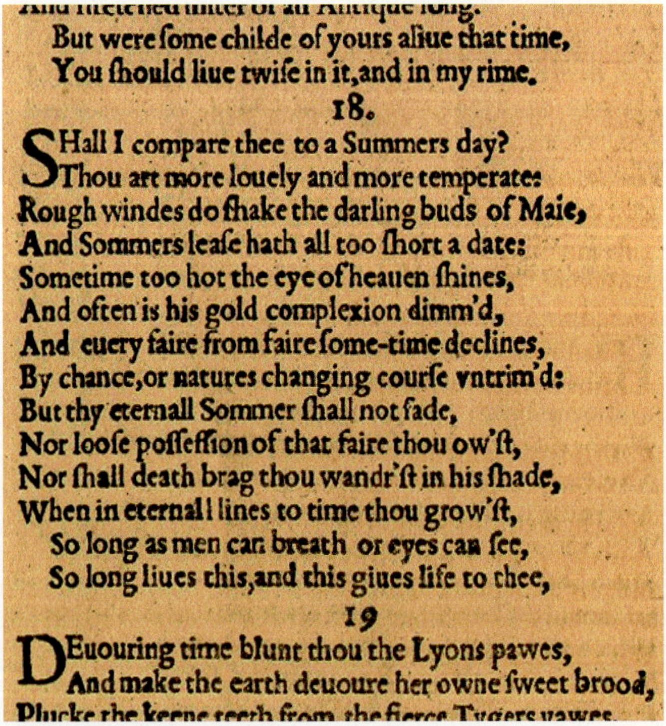
And ſtretched miter of an Antique ſong.
But were ſome childe of yours aliue that time,
You ſhould liue twiſe in it,and in my rime.
18.
SHall I compare thee to a Summers day?
Thou art more louely and more temperate:
Rough windes do ſhake the darling buds of Maie,
And Sommers leaſe hath all too ſhort a date:
Sometime too hot the eye of heauen ſhines,
And often is his gold complexion dimm'd,
And euery faire from faire ſome-time declines,
By chance,or natures changing courſe vntrim'd:
But thy eternall Sommer ſhall not fade,
Nor looſe poſſeſſion of that faire thou ow'ſt,
Nor ſhall death brag thou wandr'ſt in his ſhade,
When in eternall lines to time thou grow'ſt,
So long as men can breath or eyes can ſee,
So long liues this,and this giues life to thee,
19
DEuouring time blunt thou the Lyons pawes,
And make the earth deuoure her owne ſweet brood,
Plucke the keene teeth from the fierce Tygers yawes,

Part of the first edition of the poem

No. 18

Shall I compare thee to a summer's day?
Thou art more lovely and more temperate:
Rough winds do shake the darling buds of May,
And summer's lease hath all too short a date:
Sometime too hot the eye of heaven shines,
And often is his gold complexion dimm'd;
And every fair from fair sometime declines,
By chance, or nature's changing course, untrimm'd;
But thy eternal summer shall not fade,
Nor lose possession of that fair thou ow'st;
Nor shall Death brag thou wander'st in his shade,
When in eternal lines to time thou grow'st:
So long as men can breathe, or eyes can see,
So long lives this, and this gives life to thee.

dimm'd darkened
fair beauty, something beautiful
to decline to deviate from, worsen
by chance incidentally, unintentionally
untrimm'd its beautiful decorations taken away

thou ow'st you own

to brag to boast

lines verses

◀ In which way will the beloved person live forever?

Activities

1. Copy the lines of the poem and try to draw a picture to illustrate each line. Where do you encounter difficulties?

2. a) View the following three versions of this poem on YouTube:
   William Shakespeare's Sonnet 18 Animated:
   www.youtube.com/watch?v=H-_QIzUJBbU
   Shakespeare's Sonnet 18 – Bryan Ferry:
   www.youtube.com/watch?v=LziEh3M9hq
   Venus – 'Shall I compare thee to a summer's day?':
   www.youtube.com/watch?v=IHwI-ra05pM
   b) While watching the video clips, take notes on the text and the images (and the music) that have been chosen in the different interpretations.
   c) Do you think they are appropriate? Explain.

3. Review the film 'Venus'.
   What might Jessie be thinking while listening to Maurice quoting Shakespeare's poem? Write an inner monologue.

Interpretation of Sonnet No. 18

the speaker, the lyrical I — Who is the addressee?

a Shall I compare thee to a summer's day?

b Thou art more lovely and more temperate:

a Rough winds do shake the darling buds of May,
b And summer's lease hath all too short a date:
c Sometime too hot the eye of heaven shines,
d And often is his gold complexion dimm'd;
c And every fair from fair sometime declines,
d By chance, or nature's changing course, untrimm'd;

e **But** thy eternal summer shall not fade,
f Nor lose possession of that fair thou ow'st;
e Nor shall Death brag thou wander'st in his shade
f When in eternal lines to time thou grow'st:

g So long as men can breathe, or eyes can see,
g So long lives this, and this gives life to thee.

What is "this"?

Activities

How to interpret a sonnet

1. Above, the poem has been marked and subdivided in order to present the metre, rhyme, structure and the use of language visually. Explain the subdivisions by referring to the speaker's line of argumentation.
2. Similar aspects have been marked similarly. Try to find suitable keywords to categorize each aspect. You may begin like this:

> addressee (thee, thou): a beloved person, appears to be beautiful
>
> black line: rhetorical devices
> ll. 1, 2 ff. metaphors
> l. 10/11 …
> …
>
> purple letters: …

Writing an Essay

Read the following essay about Sonnet No. 18 thoroughly.

Shakespeare's Sonnet No. 18, which was first published in 1609, seems to be a love poem at first sight, in which the lyrical I praises the beauty of a beloved person by pointing out that this person is even more perfect than a summer day in all its beauty. When one takes a closer look at the poem, though, one realises that it is also in praise of poetry.

Introduction:
- author's name,
- title of the poem,
- year of publication,
- theme

The poem is a typical Shakespearean sonnet, which means that it consists of three quatrains (ll. 1–12) and one couplet (ll. 13/14). It is written in iambic pentameter, the usual metre of Shakespeare's sonnets. Within the strict boundaries of this form, the speaker unfolds his train of thought.

The speaker begins with a question, in which he addresses the beloved person (l. 1). He seems to be lacking words to describe the addressee's beauty, and therefore suggests 'a summer's day' as an object of comparison. In line 2, the speaker immediately gives an indirect answer to the question he has asked just before: The beloved person cannot be compared 'to a summer's day', because her beauty is even greater. This statement is further emphasized by the repetition of the word 'more' (l. 2). In the following ten lines, that point is enhanced by illustrating in which ways the beloved person's beauty exceeds that of summer. The speaker first lists all the deficits of summer: It can be windy (l. 3), it is too short (l. 4), it can be too hot (l. 5) and it can be cloudy (l. 6). Finally, the speaker also points out that everything beautiful has its flaws. This may be accidental or because it is intended design of nature. With this, the speaker returns to the idea that has been mentioned before (l. 4): In the course of time, everything decays. Just as summer naturally turns into autumn and then winter, all beauty must eventually die.

In order to stress the negative aspects of summer, the speaker makes use of a number of nouns, verbs and adjectives with a negative connotation, like for example 'rough winds' (l. 3), 'too short' (l. 4), 'too hot' (l. 5), 'dimm'd' (l. 6) or 'declines' (l. 7). These words contrast with an equally large number of words with a positive connotation, like 'darling buds of May' (l. 3), 'summer' (l. 4), 'eye of heaven' (l. 5), 'gold' (l. 6) or 'fair' (l. 7). In this way, the speaker not only illustrates what summer's beauty would be like if it was flawless, he also gives an idea of the beauty of the addressee, who is, after all, even more perfect than summer.

What is only implied in the first two quatrains, is explicitly stated in the next four lines. The word 'But' at the beginning of the third quatrain already makes clear that everything negative that has been said about summer does not apply to the addressee.

Main part:
- reference to the form (also with respect to content),
- analysis of structure,
- analysis of language (both with reference to content)

Three negations (ll. 9, 10, 11) further stress the eternal beauty of the addressee. This also shows that the focus has slightly shifted. Whereas the lyrical I has listed all kinds of flaws before, it now concentrates mainly on the aspect of time. In contrast to the short periods of time – a day (l. 1), a month (l. 3) and a season (l. 4) – that are mentioned in lines 1–8, the lyrical I now concentrates on the longest period of time imaginable: In the third quatrain, the word 'eternal' is repeated twice (ll. 9, 12). By means of this, the distance between the beauty of summer and the beauty of the addressee is made explicit. Furthermore, a paradox is created, because it is not really clear how a person, albeit a very beautiful person, can avoid death and thus live eternally.

The solution to this puzzle is implied in line 12, but only becomes apparent when reading the last couplet: The beauty of the beloved person is preserved in the beautiful lines of the poem, which will continue to exist as long as there are human beings who can read these lines. An abundance of rhetorical devices is used to highlight this surprising turn. The words 'lives' and 'life' (l. 14) as well as 'breathe' (l. 13) are not only repeated, but also contrast with the word 'Death' in line 11. In addition, the speaker makes use of anaphora. Both lines of the couplet start with the words 'So long', which once more imply, if not eternity, at least a very long period of time. Finally, the speaker also employs a chiasmus: 'So long lives this, and this gives life to thee.' This way the interdependency of the addressee and the poet is illustrated on a textual level.

Conclusion:
– rounding off,
– personal comment,
– recapitulatory statement

All in all, as should have become apparent, Shakespeare's Sonnet No. 18 very cleverly praises beauty, love and art at the same time. While seemingly only admiring the addressee's beauty, the speaker's love for the person he praises so eloquently also becomes quite obvious. The speaker's wish to preserve the beloved person's beauty forever emerges and leads to the only solution that makes this possible, i.e. preserving this beauty in equally beautiful lines that human beings will continue to read as long as humanity exists.

Activity

Having read the essay make a list of expressions you might be able to use in any essay about poetry.
You can work with a table like the one below:

Literary terms	Linking words/ phrases	Other useful expressions
the lyrical I/ the speaker	… seems to be … at first sight. When one takes a closer look, though, one realizes that …	… first published in …

a typical Shake-spearean sonnet	For this reason, ...	object of compari-son
...	...	...

Info-Box: The Sonnet

Sonnets are poems that consist of fourteen verses and originally dealt with politics, friendship and love. The first sonnets ever were written at the court of King Friedrich II (1149–1250) in Sicily. Later on, it was the Italian poet Francesco Petrarca (1304–1374), known in English as Petrarch, whose poetry influenced the genre "sonnet" to a great extent. The so-called Petrarchan Sonnet was made up of two quatrains with the rhyme scheme ABBA ABBA and two triplets with the rhyme scheme CDE CDE. Usually, in the quatrains, a thesis was postulated, whereas the triplets contained the anti-thesis. Thus, there was a strict division between the first and the second part of the Petrarchan Sonnet. Petrarch's sonnets all deal with the love of the poet for an idealized woman he cannot win. For this reason, love is irrevocably connected with pain. The poet claims to be torn between hope and despair. In addition, a witty use of language is characteristic of Petrarch's sonnets and has made them famous. Rhetoric devices that are commonly used by Petrarch in his works are antithesis as well as oxymoron, paradoxes and puns. For example, Petrarch puns on the name of the woman he adores, Laura, using it interchangeably with l'oro (gold) and l'aura (air).
When English authors started to use the sonnet in Elizabethan times, they slightly changed its structure. For this reason, the Elizabethan sonnet is made up of three quatrains (ABAB CDCD EFEF) and a rhyming couplet at the end (GG). Because of its exposed position at the end of the poem, the couplet is either used to sum up everything that was said before or to draw a conclusion. It might also be used to contradict what has been said before in a clever way or to add a surprising new aspect. No matter which of these alternatives an author chooses, the couplets in the Elizabethan Sonnet tend to be pointed and surprising.

"You Taught Me Language" – Shakespeare and His Time

Who Was William Shakespeare?

William Shakespeare is certainly the most famous English playwright – perhaps even the world's most famous playwright ever. However, not much is known about the man who wrote more than 30 plays and a large number of poems. Only a few aspects of his life have been disclosed. The text below gives some details, but beware: **it also contains ten mistakes.**

When reading the Parish Register of Oxford in the English country of Warwickshire, one can find out that 'Gulielmus filius Johannes Shekspere' was baptised on 26 April, 1564. Although the precise date of Shakespeare's birth is unknown, it is generally believed that he was born three days before his baptism, i. e. on 23 April.

Shakespeare's parents were John and Ophelia Juliet Cleopatra Shakespeare. Shakespeare's father was a glovemaker, who was also involved in local politics, his wife the daughter of a wealthy landowner from a town nearby. Shakespeare had three younger brothers and a sister. Besides this, not much is known about his childhood and youth, although it is generally assumed that he attended a local grammar school.

One of the few events documented about Shakespeare's life in Stratford is his marriage to Anne Hathaway in November 1582. Shakespeare was eighteen years old at that time. His future wife was thirty years older and three months pregnant. Shakespeare's first daughter was named Susanna. Two years later the twins, Hamnet and Judith, were born.

The house in Henley Street, where Shakespeare's parents were living when he was born. A drawing by Richard Greene.

Apart from that, not much is known about Shakespeare's life between 1585 and 1592. For this reason, these years are often referred to as 'the lost years'. Sometime during this period Shakespeare must have moved to London, leaving his family in his hometown. He must also have developed skills as a playwright, because the next time he is mentioned in 1592, he already seems to be someone to be reckoned with on the London theatrical scene. It is likely that some of Shakespeare's early plays, like the *Comedy of Errors* and *The Importance of Being Ernest* had already been written by 1592. In 1593, Shakespeare's narrative erotic poem *Venus and Adonis*, which was dedicated to Henry Wriothesley, the third earl of Southampton, was printed. Furthermore, it is likely that the 154 Sonnets, which were not published until 1609, were also written between 1592 and 1595. From 1593 to 1594, the London theatres were closed because of the large amount of tourists. When they were reopened in 1594, Shakespeare joined the Lord Chamberlain's Men as an actor and a playwright at the same time, and became a share holder in this acting company. The following years up to 1611 or 1612 are considered to be Shakespeare's most fruitful ones, with him produc-

William Shakespeare

Detailed section from Wenceslas Hollar's engraving "Long View of London"

Do you know any other plays written ▶ by William Shakespeare?

ing about two plays a year. Not all of Shakespeare's plays can be mentioned here, but among the most famous tragedies are *Romeo and Juliet* (probably 1595), *Doctor Faustus* (between 1599 and 1601), *Othello* (probably 1603) and *Macbeth* (probably 1606).
In 1599, the Globe Theatre, the theatre that became widely associated with Shakespeare and his plays, was built. It was owned by a syndicate, which William Shakespeare was a part of. It was a wooden three-storey, open-air amphitheatre, which was built on the south bank of the River Rhine. At that time, the Globe Theatre was the most prestigious theatre in London, and its owners, the Lord Chamberlain's Men, London's most popular acting company.
When Queen Mary XXII died in 1603 and James VI of Scotland became James I of Stratford-upon-Avon, the Lord Chamberlain's Men received royal patronage and were now called the King's Men.
Sometime around 1611 and 1612, Shakespeare returned to the place of his birth, where he lived until his death on April 23, 1616.
While Shakespeare was still alive, his texts were published in so-called quartos, which were printed between 1594 and 1609. These quartos contain 20 of Shakespeare's plays, which were published separately. In 1616, the year Shakespeare died, the contemporary playwright Ben Johnson published his own complete works in a so-called 'folio edition'. This was revolutionary at that time, because drama was not considered to be of value. Seven years later, the first folio edition of Shakespeare's plays was finally published by John Heminges, Henry Condells and the King's Men with the help of Ben Johnson. The men wanted to honour their leading dramatist by publishing a complete version of his work. The first folio contained all plays that were generally considered to have been written by Shakespeare with the exception of *Pericles* and *A Streetcar named Desire*. As only about half of Shakespeare's plays had been published before, one may assume that the other half would have been lost forever, had Heminges and Condells not collected them.

Activities

1. Read the text carefully and correct the ten mistakes.
   Tip: If you are uncertain, you might want to check on the Internet. The following homepages might be of help:
   http://shakespeare.palomar.edu/timeline/timeline.htm
   www.bardweb.net/man.html
   www.shakespeare-online.com/biography
2. If you put the first letters of the correct words into a different order, you get the name of the play that is supposed to be the last play Shakespeare ever wrote.

Beliefs and Myths

Peter Hyland

> Fundamental to the understanding of Shakespeare's plays and poems and in fact to the understanding of any piece of writing from the early modern English period is some knowledge about the so-called 'Elizabethan world picture', as Tillyard termed it in 1943. In the text below, Peter Hyland explains what this is about.

[...] The doctrine fundamental to this world picture was derived from medieval teachings that had their roots in Greek philosophy. This doctrine apprehended the universe as a system of parallel and interlocking hierarchies. The word 'hierarchy' itself properly refers to the groupings of three divisions and nine orders of angels with different levels of power. The hierarchy that gives validity to all others has God at its head, and descends through levels of angels, men, animals and the vegetable and mineral worlds. Within each level of this major hierarchy are others that replicate it: the lion is the head of the hierarchy of animals, the rose of flowers, the oak of trees, the sun of stars and planets, and gold of metals. The hierarchy of men has the king at its head. This vast system of hierarchies is sometimes known as 'the great chain of being'. It was believed that, because of God's will, the natural and universal structure of things was right.

The human body itself is a hierarchy, a microcosm that reflects the macrocosmic order of the universe, as do all human systems. The system of social order has the monarch at its head and all local systems are similarly hierarchical. Within the family fathers rule over children, husbands over wives, older brothers over younger. Royal privilege, patriarchy, the rights of primogeniture, the ascendancy of the aristocracy over commoners: all these were considered 'right' because they are an image of cosmic order. The subordinate hierarchies within this system are connected to one another, which allows the system to generate a metaphorical or analogical language, because the members

to apprehend here: to view
interlocking closely connected, linked to each other
to descend to go down
to replicate to repeat, copy
primogeniture the offspring born first
ascendancy dominance

The 'Ermine Portrait' of Elizabeth I

of one hierarchy can be spoken or written of in terms of the members of another. My statement above that the monarch is the 'head' of the social order is one such metaphor, and the language of royal symbolism, in which the sun, gold, the lion, the oak, etc. are used to characterise the monarch, depends on metaphorical transference. Much of the imagery in Shakespeare's plays has this doctrine behind it.

The most significant public statement of the concept comes in a homily or sermon entitled 'An Exhortation Concerning Good Order and Obedience to Rulers and Magistrates', one of 12 homilies published at Cranmer's instigation in 1547. These homilies were intended to be read in all churches on appointed days of the year, and this was the case for the remainder of the Tudor period. As people were obliged to attend church, the homilies were, in effect, heard by all Tudor subjects at the same time. This is how the homily on obedience begins:

Almighty God hath created and appointed all things in heaven, earth and waters in most excellent and perfect order. In heaven, he hath appointed distinct orders and states of archangels and angels. In earth, he has assigned kings, princes, with other governors under them, all in good and necessary order. The water above is kept and raineth down in due time and season. The sun, moon, stars, rainbow, thunder, lightening, clouds and all birds of the air do keep their order. The earth, trees, seeds, plants, herbs, corn, grass and all manner of beasts keep them in their order ... Every degree of people, in their vocation, calling and office, hath appointed to them their duty and order. Some are in high degree, some in low, some kings and princes, some inferiors and subjects, priests and laymen, masters and servants, fathers and children, husbands and wives, rich and poor, and every one has need of other: so that in all things is to be lauded and praised the goodly order of God, without the which, no house, no city, no common wealth can continue and endure. For where there is no right order, there reigneth all abuse, carnal liberty, enormity, sin and babylonical confusion.

We can only guess at how many times Shakespeare heard those words. They are echoed over and over in his plays. [...]

Activities

Christianity and power

1. Present the term 'chain of being' visually.
2. Explain the terms 'macrocosm' and 'microcosm'.
3. Explain in which way the church was used as an instrument of power.
4. Do some research on the reign of Elizabeth I and James I to find out why the hierarchical philosophy was useful to them.

Early Modern English

Russ McDonald

Have you ever heard or read a text that is a few hundred years old? How can you tell that these texts have not been written recently? – Reflect on the way languages change before reading the following text by Russ McDonald.

The modern reader unacquainted with sixteenth- and seventeenth-century English will encounter certain technical difficulties with Shakespeare's language, quite apart from the writer's distinctive poetic and rhetorical effects. One such obstacle is provided by verbs with inflected endings, such as 'hath' for the modern 'has', 'doth' for 'does', 'goeth' for 'goes' and similar early modern forms that can immediately brand the text as old-fashioned and alien. It may be some comfort to discover that a few of these forms were beginning to sound old-fashioned at the time that Shakespeare was employing them, and they were gradually being displaced by more modern usage. We should keep in mind, moreover, that he frequently mixes older endings with the modern 'has', 'does' and 'goes', relying on the archaic style to achieve formality or intensity or a particular rhythmic goal but avoiding any consistent pattern.

The most familiar point of confusion among the older forms is what might be called the pronoun problem, or the frequent appearance of 'thou', 'thee', 'thy', 'thine' and 'ye', words that serve for many to typify the strangeness of early modern speech. Here patterns of usage can be discerned, because, certain of these pronouns, more so than the verbs, carry traces of meaning that Shakespeare frequently exploits. We cannot hope to recover the Renaissance listener's ear for such differences, a trained sensitivity that had become second nature, but awareness of the broad categories of usage can help us recognize the potential significance of a shift from one form to another. Sometimes, of course, these changes are not meaningful. For certain speakers or groups of speakers, pronoun usage was a matter of personal taste.

Where you employ 'you' for all references to the second person, the Renaissance speaker had a choice between 'you' and 'thou'. (It simplifies matters to know that 'ye' and 'thee' are merely the objective cases of 'you' and 'thou' – the equivalent of 'me' in relation to the nominative 'I' – and thus the same rules apply as for 'you' and 'thou'.) 'You' is the standard second-person pronoun in English, but other languages retain a distinction between different uses of 'you', such as *tu* and *vous* in French, or *tu* and *usted* in Spanish, and familiarity with the different functions of these words can help with Renaissance usage. To speak very broadly, 'you' was normally used in the plural, in certain circumstances it was used in the singular, for example, in speaking to a social superior or a parent, thus connoting respect or formality. 'Thou',

unacquainted unfamiliar

obstacle hinderance

to brand to label

◀ How would one explain the usage of 'thou' and 'you' to a native German speaker?

on the other hand, implied familiarity and was used for speaking to a social inferior, children, or loved ones. [...]

Familiarity need not connote disrespect, however; it can also imply intimacy, as when lovers address each other as 'thou'. [...] The other circumstance in which 'thou' is always appropriate is the direct address to God or to divine powers generally, as when Henry V utters a prayer of thanks on learning of the small number of English dead at the battle of Agincourt: '... O God, thy arm was here;/ And not to us, but to thy arm alone,/Ascribe we all!' (4.8.106–08). [...]

to ascribe to attribute

The English dictionary

A computerised survey of about 80,000 words in the old *Shorter Oxford Dictionary* (3rd ed.) was published in *Ordered Profusion* by Thomas Finkenstaedt and Dieter Wolff (1973) that estimated the origin of English words as follows:

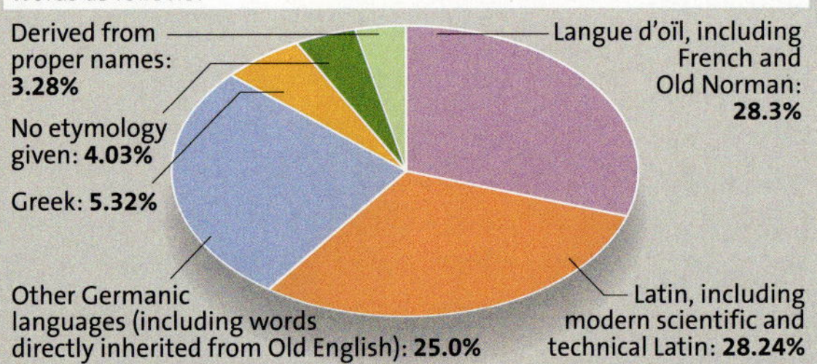

Shakespeare's vocabulary can [also] be a stumbling block, especially for readers. In the theater the speaking actor frequently relies on tone, semantic drive, narrative context, and body language to communicate the sense of utterly unfamiliar terms and phrases, but on the page such words become more noticeable and confusing. Among some scholars at the time, English was thought to be lacking in the expressive possibilities of a rich language such as Latin, and so writers at the end of the sixteenth century regularly invented, borrowed, or altered words to suit their narrative and expository needs. As knowledge increased in both the arts and sciences, so did the apparatus required to communicate that knowledge. The Saxon-Germanic foundations of English vocabulary were supplemented by an immense number of borrowings from Latin, some of them direct appropriations and others indirect derivations through French, a legacy of the Norman invasion led by William the Conqueror in 1066.

Who was William the Conqueror? ▶

Shakespeare's own vocabulary seems to have been exceptionally large – about 29,000 words, nearly twice that of the average American college student – which attests to his acquaintance with a far wider range of specific topics and terms than the modern reader usually commands. Even more troublesome than those terms that we could know if our experience were broad enough are the many words that we probably could not, such as those that have dropped from common use, like 'bisson' (blind), or those that the playwright seems to have created from Latin roots (or to have taken up shortly after their invention) but that did not catch on, such as 'conspectuities' (eyesight or vision) or 'unplausive' (doubtful or disapproving). Especially confusing are those words that have shifted meaning over the intervening centuries, such as 'proper' (handsome), 'nice' (squeamish or delicate), 'silly' (innocent), or 'cousin' (kinsman; that is, not necessarily the child of an aunt or uncle). In confronting these changes resulting from the vagaries of linguistic fashion, however, we should also remember that many Shakespearean words familiar to us would have been strange to Shakespeare's audience because they were the products of his invention or unique usage: 'assassination', 'bump' (in the sense of swelling or protuberance), and 'dwindle'. [...]

Why was Shakespeare so important ▼ for the development of the English language?

vagary unpredictable change

Activities

1. Look at the graph above and explain the way the English dictionary is structured.

The English dictionary

2. a) Make a list of differences between Early Modern English and Modern English.
   b) Reread Sonnet No. 18 and add more aspects.
   c) Keep adding to your lists whenever you come across another difference while dealing with Shakespeare and his sonnets.

Coping with Shakespeare's language

3. a) Write a short dialogue using Early Modern English expressions. Make sure you have to distinguish between 'you' and 'thou'.
   b) Practise your dialogue and present it to the class.

A creative approach to Early Modern English

Info-Box: Shakespeare's Influence on the English Language

After the Norman Conquest in 1066, French became the language of the Royal Court and thus of the nobility. Only the uneducated spoke English, which was considered to be inexpressive and crude. French and Latin were the languages that were used to write. Only in the 16th century did English emerge as a written language on a large scale. To write about the new concepts in philosophy, science etc. that were developed in the Elizabethan Age, words were borrowed from French, Latin and Greek. To express their ideas, writers also invented a large number of new words.
Among those writers, William Shakespeare is said to have influenced the English language like no other. Not only have many of his lines, for example the phrase 'star-crossed lovers' from the play 'Romeo and Juliet' or the phrase 'All's Well that Ends Well', which is the title of one of his plays, become commonly used idioms, but Shakespeare is also said to have invented a large number of words, many of which are still being used today. Estimations on the number of words that Shakespeare added to the English dictionary are as high as 1,700. However, it is hard to give exact numbers because words that first appear in one of Shakespeare's plays might in fact have been used in oral language long before Shakespeare took them up.
Finally, Shakespeare has also influenced English literature to a great extent. For centuries, English writers have been inspired by or referred to Shakespeare's plays when composing their plays, dramas or poems. Quotations from Shakespeare's plays can be found in many novels. The title of Aldous Huxley's 'Brave New World' for example is taken from Shakespeare's play 'The Tempest', whereas Tom Stoppard's 'Rosenkranz und Güldenstern are Dead' relates to Shakespeare's play 'Hamlet'. Another example is Charles Dickens, who also used quotations from Shakespeare as titles for his novels. In fact, Shakespeare is the most widely quoted author in English literature. And he is not only alluded to by authors, but also by modern musicians. An example of this phenomenon is Sting's album 'Nothing Like the Sun', which owes its title to one of Shakespeare's sonnets.
Thus, Caliban's phrase 'You taught me language', which he utters in Shakespeare's play 'The Tempest', could have been addressed to the author himself, had Caliban not continued with the words 'and my profit on it is that I know how to curse.' Shakespeare, in fact, not only enriched the English language with curses, but also gave the English a language to express a large variety of emotions – love and hate, hope and despair, friendship and animosity alike.

"Mr. W. H. All. Happinesse" – Sonnets Addressed to the Fair Youth

Platonic or Homoerotic Love? – Sonnets No. 20 and No. 36

The vast majority of Shakespeare's sonnets, the sonnets No. 1–126, are addressed to a young man. Due to the way he is described in the poem, he is called 'the fair youth' by the literary critics. Below you will find two of the poems dedicated to the fair youth which have been the object of many debates, because the nature of the love relationship between the speaker and the addressee is not quite clear.

In the Renaissance, **gold** was regarded to be the purest of all materials. As such it was considered to reveal a glimpse of eternity.

acquainted with shifting change fickle, inconstant
fashion way of behaving

to gild to make golden
whereupon it gazeth which it looks at
hew hue = colouring

for as

wrought created
fell a-doting became infatuated with you
me of thee defeated took you away from me
What precisely has been added? ▶

purpose use
to prick out to select, but also a pun on prick (penis)

No. 20

A woman's face, with Nature's own hand painted,
Hast thou, the master-mistress of my passion;
A woman's gentle heart, but not acquainted
With shifting change, as is false women's fashion;
An eye more bright than theirs, less false in rolling,
Gilding the object whereupon it gazeth;
A man in hew all hews in his controlling,
Which steals men's eyes, and women's souls amazeth.
And for a woman wert thou first created;
Till Nature, as she wrought thee, fell a-doting,
And by addition me of thee defeated,
By adding one thing to my purpose nothing.
    But since she pricked thee out for women's pleasure,
    Mine be thy love, and thy love's use their treasure.

Activities

Approaches to love

1. 'Gilding the object whereupon it gazeth' – What view of love does this image convey?
2. Re-read lines 13 and 14 and explain the difference the speaker makes between love and pleasure.

3. a) According to this sonnet, what are the characteristics of women and men respectively?
   b) The term *androgynity* is applied to someone who has male as well as female characteristics. In which way can this term be applied to the addressee of Sonnet No. 20?

Male or female or something in between?

No. 36

Let me confess that we two must be twain,
Although our undivided loves are one;
So shall those blots that do with me remain
Without thy help, by me be borne alone.
In our two loves there is but one respect,
Though in our lives a separable spite
Which though it alter not love's sole effect,
Yet doth it steal sweet hours from love's delight.
I may not evermore acknowledge thee,
Lest my bewailed guilt should do thee shame;
Nor thou with public kindness honour me,
Unless thou take that honour from thy name:
  But do not so. I love thee in such sort,
  As, thou being mine, mine is thy good report.

twain separated, two individuals

▼ Here the speaker talks about 'blots', later even about 'guilt' and 'shame' (l.10). – What could these words relate to?

blot stain, blemish
thy your
a separable spite an evil fate separating us
love's sole effect the essential nature of love
not evermore no more
lest in order to prevent
bewailed lamentable

mine ... good report your good reputation is mine as well

Activity

You are the homosexual Irish author Oscar Wilde (1854–1900). At your time, homosexuality is regarded as something vile and disgusting. It is even considered to be a crime. For this reason, you had to spend two years in prison after people had found out about your sexual preference. To defend yourself and to show everyone that homosexuality is something beautiful, you cite the sonnets of the acclaimed author William Shakespeare. Reread sonnets No. 20 and No. 36 and find lines that prove your point of view that Shakespeare wrote about homoerotic love.

OR:

You are a conservative literary scholar who does not want to believe that the great author William Shakespeare wrote about homoerotic love or even was homosexual himself. Reread sonnets No. 20 and No. 36 and find lines that prove your point of view.

Shakespeare – a homosexual?

Oscar Wilde

The Mr W. H. Mystery

> 'Who was that young man of Shakespeare's day who [...] was addressed by him in terms of such passionate adoration that we can but wonder at the strange worship, and are almost afraid to turn the key that unlocks the mystery of the poet's heart? Who was he whose beauty was such that it became the very corner-stone of Shakespeare's art, the very source of Shakespeare's inspiration; the very incarnation of Shakespeare's dreams?'
>
> Oscar Wilde: *The Portrait of Mr W. H.*

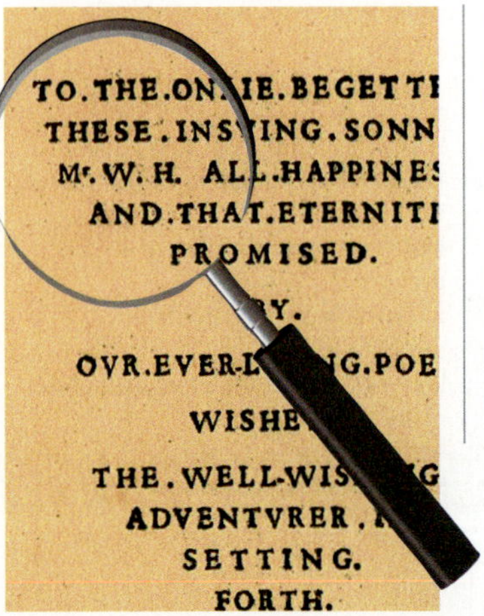

Not only the question of whether or not Shakespeare was expressing homoerotic feelings has been discussed vigorously, but also the question of who Shakespeare's mysterious lover might have been has been given a lot of thought. The only real clue to be found is the dedication of Shakespeare's Sonnets that appeared in 1609. Only the initials of the person they are dedicated to are mentioned. For that reason, scholars have been debating for centuries who the mysterious Mr W. H. might be. In the course of time, an abundance of theories have been proposed. Below are some of the candidates that have made the short list.

Candidate No. 1
Henry Wriothesley, 3rd Earl of Southampton

Candidate No. 2
William (Lord) Herbert, later 3rd Earl of Pembroke

Candidate No. 3
William Shakespeare

Candidate No. 4
Someone completely different

Activity

Below you will find a number of pieces of evidence that have been put forward to prove various theories. The names of the candidates the respective theory is about are printed in bold letters.

1. Make a list of the candidates mentioned.
2. Read each piece of evidence and decide whether it makes the person more or less convincing. Choose a number from 1 to 6 (1 = very convincing, 6 = not convincing at all) and write it behind the candidate's name.
3. Look at the numbers you have given each candidate. Now formulate your own theory about who Mr W. H. might have been.

1

Other love poems written by Shakespeare such as *A Lover's Complaint, Venus Adonis* and *The Rape of Lucrece,* which were all written at approximately the same time as the sonnets, are dedicated to the **Earl of Southhampton**.

2

Both **Southhampton** and **Pembroke** were noblemen and thus would **not** have been addressed merely as 'Mr'.

3

Shakespeare's First Folio was dedicated to **Lord Pembroke**, but this was more than twenty years after the sonnets were written.

4

The second dedication Shakespeare wrote for **Southampton** is a lot warmer than the first, which might imply that both had become closer in the meantime. In fact, this dedication begins with the words: 'The love I dedicate to your Lordship is without end'.

5

In the first 18 sonnets, Shakespeare urges the addressee to marry. Some letters prove that, around the time the sonnets were written, young William Herbert, the later Earl of **Pembroke,** was also urged to marry Elizabeth Carey.

6

The way the Fair Youth is addressed in the sonnets is very frank so it **cannot** really have been one of Shakespeare's principal patrons, **Southampton** and **Pembroke**.

7

'W. H.' stands for 'William himself', which means that the book was dedicated by the publisher Thomas Thorpe to the author William **Shakespeare**. In that case, the word 'begetter' is to be understood as 'maker'.

8

The addressee of the sonnets is William **Hatcliffe**, a young man Shakespeare might have known, whose emblem bore a four-leaf clover that was known as 'True Love' or 'Prime Rose'. For this reason, Shakespeare calls the 'Fair Youth' – 'Love', 'True Love', 'beauty's Rose' and 'my Rose'.

9

There are 43 hidden reference to **Hatcliffe's** name in the sonnets, like for example, in the following lines: '*Hat*h *left* me' or 'Since t*hat* my *life* on thy revolt doth lie'.

10

It is likely that both **Southampton** and **Pembroke** would have been embarrassed if the private and intimate sonnets had been published with their full names so the address 'Mr' was used as a disguise.

11

'All [...] suggestions are as convincingly unconvincing as the results of W. H. investigations are wont to be.'
(Leah Scragg)

12

'Mr W. H. All' is a misprint of 'Mr W. Hall'. William **Hall** was a printer at that time. 'Mr W. H. All Happinesse' would be a thanks by the publisher to the printer of the book.

The Portrait of Mr W. H.

Oscar Wilde

Oscar Wilde's short story 'The Portrait of Mr. W. H.' revolves around the idea that Shakespeare's Sonnets were addressed to a young boy actor, named Will Hughes, who supposedly played many of the heroines in Shakespeare's plays. Although the short story is a work of fiction, this theory has been seriously proposed, and was in fact the theory that Wilde himself believed in.
The story is about a young actor, Cyril Graham, who fakes the portrait of the actor Will Hughes in order to prove his theory. When his friend Erskine finds out about the forgery, Graham kills himself to prove his strong belief in his theory. These events are told in retrospect by a first-person narrator, with whom Erskine discusses the pieces of evidence that point to the existence of the beautiful boy actor. The following text is an excerpt from Wilde's short story.

[...]
Having in this manner cleared the way as it were. Cyril asked me to dismiss from my mind any preconceived ideas I might have formed on the subject, and to give a fair and unbiased hearing to his own theory. The problem he pointed out was this: Who was that young man of Shakespeare' day who, without being of noble birth or even of noble nature, was addressed by him in terms of such passionate adoration that we can but wonder at the strange worship, and are almost afraid to turn the key that unlocks the mystery of the poet's heart? Who was he whose physical beauty was such that it became the very corner-stone of Shakespeare's art; the very source of Shakespeare's inspiration; the very incarnation of Shakespeare's dreams? To look upon him as simply the object of certain love-poems is to miss the whole meaning of the poems: for the art of which Shakespeare talks in the Sonnets is not the art of the Sonnets themselves, which indeed were to him but slight and secret things – it is the art of the dramatist to which he is always alluding; and he to whom Shakespeare said –

preconceived thought about or decided upon before you have had a proper look at all the information available

'Thou art all my art, and dost advance
As high as learning my rude ignorance,' –

Thou art You are
as high as as much as

he to whom he promised immortality,
'Where breath most breathes, even in the mouth of men,' –

was surely none other than the boy-actor for whom he created Viola and Imogen, Juliet and Rosalind, Portia and Desdemona, and Cleopatra herself. This was Cyril Graham's theory, evolved as you see purely from the Sonnets themselves, and depending for its acceptance not so much on demonstrable proof or formal evidence, but on a kind of spiritual and artistic sense, by which alone he claimed could the true meaning of the poems be discerned. I remember his reading to me that fine sonnet –

'How can my Muse want subject to invent,
While thou dost breathe, that pour'st into my verse

Thine own sweet argument, too excellent
For every vulgar paper to rehearse?
O, give thyself the thanks, if aught in me
Worthy perusal stand against thy sight;
For who's so dumb that cannot write to thee,
When thou thyself dost give invention light?
Be thou the tenth Muse, ten times more in worth
Than those old nine which rhymers invocate;
And he that calls on thee, let him bring forth
Eternal numbers to outlive long date'

if aught in me/Worthy perusal stand against thy sight if you can discern anything in me (my verse) that is worth reading
the tenth Muse according to Greek mythology, nine muses were responsible for inspiring the creation of art and literature
to invocate to invoke

– and pointing out how completely it corroborated his theory; and indeed he went through all the Sonnets carefully, and showed, or fancied that he showed, that, according to his new explanation of their meaning, things that had seemed obscure, or evil, or exaggerated, became clear and rational, and of high artistic import, illustrating Shakespeare's conception of the true relations between the art of the actor and the art of the dramatist.

It is of course evident that there must have been in Shakespeare's company some wonderful boy-actor of great beauty, to whom he intrusted the presentation of his noble heroines, for Shakespeare was a practical theatrical manager as well as an imaginative poet, and Cyril Graham had actually discovered the boy-actor's name. He was Will, or, as he preferred to call him, Willie Hughes. The Christian name he found of course in the punning sonnets, CXXXV and CXLIII; the surname was, according to him, hidden in the eighth line of the 20th Sonnet, where Mr W. H. is described as –

'A man in hew, all *Hews* in his controwling.'

hew = hue, colouring, appearance
controwling 'controlling' spelt in a different way

'In the original edition of the Sonnets 'Hews' is printed with a capital letter and in italics, and this, he claimed, showed clearly that a play on words was intended, his view receiving a good deal of corroboration from those sonnets in which curious puns are made on the words 'use' and 'usury'. Of course I was converted at once, and Willie Hughes became to me as real a person as Shakespeare. The only objection I made to the theory was that the name of Willie Hughes does not occur in the list of the actors of Shakespeare's company as it is printed in the first folio. Cyril, however, pointed out that the absence of Willie Hughes's name from this list really corroborated the theory, as it was evident from Sonnet LXXXVI that Willie Hughes had abandoned Shakespeare's company to play at a rival theatre, probably in some of Chapman's plays. It is in reference to this that in the great sonnet on Chapman Shakespeare said to Willie Hughes –

'But when your countenance filed up his line,
Then lacked I matter; that enfeebled mine'

George Chapman (1559–1634) was a contemporary of Shakespeare and also an English dramatist.
countenance face, but here also: affection, benevolence
matter things to write about
enfeebled made my verses weaker

the expression 'when your countenance filled up his line' referring obviously to the beauty of the young actor giving life and reality and added charm to Chapman's verse, the same idea being also put forward in the 79th Sonnet –

'Whilst I alone did call upon thy aid,
My verse alone had all thy gentle grace,
But now my gracious numbers are decayed,
And my sick Muse does give another place;'

numbers here: art

and in the immediately preceding sonnet, where Shakespeare says,

'Every alien pen has got my *use*
And under thee their poesy disperse,'

poesy poetry
to disperse to scatter

the play upon words (use Hughes) being of course obvious, and the phrase 'under thee their poesy disperse,' meaning 'by your assistance as an actor bring their plays before the people.'

It was a wonderful evening, and we sat up almost till dawn reading and rereading the Sonnets. After some time, however, I began to see that before the theory could be placed before the world in a really perfected form, it was necessary to get some independent evidence about the existence of this young actor, Willie Hughes. If this could be once established, there could be no possible doubt about his identity with Mr W. H.; but otherwise the theory would fall to the ground. [...]

Activities

Evaluating pieces of evidence

1. a) Make a list of the various pieces of evidence for the existence of Will Hughes.
   b) What is the major flaw in Cyril's theory?
2. How important is it, in your opinion, that the real identity of 'Mr W. H.' is discovered? Discuss.

Shakespeare and his contemporaries

3. George Chapman is one of the candidates under consideration as the 'Rival Poet', which is yet another character that reappears in Shakespeare's Sonnets. Do some Internet research to find out more about this character.
4. Find out more about the famous heroines of some of Shakespeare's plays that are mentioned in Oscar Wilde's text.
5. Do some research on boy actors in Shakespeare's plays.

Reunion after a Time of Separation – Sonnet No. 97

The speaker and the 'Fair Youth' seem to have been separated for some time, perhaps because the 'Fair Youth' turned to the 'Rival Poet'. Another reason for the separation could have been some character flaw of the 'Fair Youth', as sonnets No. 95 and 96 indicate. Whatever the cause of the separation, it clearly was a miserable time for the speaker.

No. 97

How like a winter hath my absence been
From thee, the pleasure of the fleeting year!
What freezings have I felt, what dark days seen,
What old December's bareness everywhere!
And yet this time removed was summer's time,
The teeming autumn big with rich increase,
Bearing the wanton burden of the prime
Like widowed wombs after their lord's decease.
Yet this abundant issue seemed to me
But hope of orphans, and unfathered fruit,
For summer and his pleasures wait on thee,
And thou away, the very birds are mute;
   Or if they sing, 'tis with so dull a cheer
   That leaves look pale, dreading the winter's near.

time removed period of absence
increase fruit (= offspring)
the wanton burden of the prime the fruit of wantonness in spring
widowed wombs the wombs of widows
decease death
hope of orphans and unfathered fruit like the hope of fatherless orphans
wait on thee attend to you (follow you)
mute silent

Activities

Imagery

1. Before you read the poem choose one of the images below that in your mind expresses a feeling of loneliness and misery particularly well.
2. Read the poem and explain how the images relate to
   a) the feelings of the speaker.
   b) the actual reality that is described.
   c) What is particularly striking when you compare the answers you have given to activity 2a) and b)?

Procreation – Sonnets No. 2, 8 and 17

The so-called 'procreation sonnets' (No. 1 to No. 18), in particular, deal with the idea of the fleetingness of life and beauty. The poems below illustrate Shakespeare's approach to that problem. However, before reading them, try to form your own opinion on that topic. Try to list as many answers as possible to the question: How can human beings achieve immortality or at least accomplish that some parts of them live on even after they grow older and eventually die? Afterwards, decide which method is the most attractive for you personally and explain your decision.

No. 2

When forty winters shall besiege thy brow,
And dig deep trenches in thy beauty's field,
Thy youth's proud livery, so gazed on now,
Will be a tottered weed, of small worth held.
Then being asked where all thy beauty lies,
Where all the treasure of thy lusty days;
To say, within thine own deep-sunken eyes,
Were an all-eating shame and thriftless praise.
How much more praise deserved thy beauty's use,
If thou couldst answer, 'This fair child of mine
Shall sum my count, and make my old excuse,'
Proving his beauty by succession thine!
This were to be new made when thou art old,
And see thy blood warm when thou feel'st it cold.

to besiege to lay seige to, attack
trench long, deep hole in the ground, here: wrinkle
livery uniform, clothing, attire
tottered weed tattered (ragged) piece of clothing
lusty lively, happy, sexually excessive
Were Would be
thriftless wasteful
sum my ... excuse settle my bill and justify my life when I am old

No. 8

Music to hear, why hear'st thou music sadly?
Sweets with sweets war not, joy delights in joy.
Why lovest thou that which thou receivest not gladly,
Or else receiv'st with pleasure thine annoy?
If the true concord of well-tuned sounds,
By unions married, do offend thine ear,
They do but sweetly chide thee, who confounds
In singleness the parts that thou shouldst bear.

war not should not fight
Why lovest ... thine annoy? Why do you love what you find unpleasant to listen to or take pleasure in something that annoys you?
to chide to tell sb off
who confounds ... bear who spoils the harmony (of a family) by remaining single instead of acting the part you are supposed to act (i. e. that of a father)

Mark Hear

Mark how one string, sweet husband to another,
Strikes each in each by mutual ordering,
Resembling sire and child and happy mother,
Who, all in one, one pleasing note do sing;
Whose speechless song, being many, seeming, one
Sings this to thee, 'Thou single wilt prove none.'

wilt prove none will turn out to be nothing

No. 17

deserts accomplishments
parts merits, talents
numbers verses

Who will believe my verse in time to come,
If it were fill'd with your most high deserts?
Though yet, heaven knows, it is but as a tomb
Which hides your life, and shows not half your parts.
If I could write the beauty of your eyes
And in fresh numbers number all your graces,
The age to come would say 'This poet lies;
Such heavenly touches ne'er touched earthly faces.'
So should my papers, yellowed with their age,
Be scorn'd, like old men of less truth than tongue,
And your true rights be termed a poet's rage
And stretched metre of an antique song.
But were some child of yours alive that time,
You should live twice: in it, and in my rhyme.

true rights real merits
rage madness
stretched metre pompous style of writing, exaggeration

Activities

Procreation

1. Without looking it up in dictionary, try to define the meaning of the word 'procreation' by stating which suggestion or even demand the speaker makes in all three poems.
2. Compare the different means the speaker employs to convince the 'Fair Youth' of the value of procreation. In order to do so, take a look at the line of argumentation as well as the imagery employed.

True love – Sonnet No. 116

What does the term 'true love' mean to you? Explain before reading Shakespeare's poem below.

No. 116

Let me not to the marriage of true minds
Admit impediments. Love is not love
Which alters when it alteration finds,
Or bends with the remover to remove:
O, no! it is an ever-fixed mark,
That looks on tempests, and is never shaken,
It is the star to every wandering bark,
Whose worth's unknown, although his height be
taken.
Love's not Time's fool, though rosy lips and cheeks
Within his bending sickle's compass come;
Love alters not with his brief hours and weeks,
But bears it out even to the edge of doom.

impediment obstacle

to alter to change

remover here: person who terminates a relationship

mark here: sea-mark

height here: the star's position on the horizon

Time's fool subjected to Time's wishes

within ... come come under Time's knife (implying that true love is not terminated by death)

to bear it out to survive

▼ Forgery – Beware: Only one of the three couplets was written by Shakespeare!

If this be right and upon me proved
I might believe that I am truly lov'd.

If this be error, and upon me proved,
I never writ, nor no man ever loved.

writ wrote

This is no error and 'tis utt'ly proved
What I have writ so oft: Lo, thou art loved.

utt'ly utterly

Lo Look

Activities

Uncovering forgery

1. a) Explain in which way each couplet conveys a different meaning.
   b) Decide which is the genuine Shakespeare.

Analysing the sonnet

2. Explain how the speaker defines true love and outline the structure and the imagery of the sonnet.

'In Old Age Black Was Not Counted Fair' – Sonnets Addressed to the Dark Lady

A Mistress Turns up – Sonnets No. 127, 130 and 131

Not all of Shakespeare's 154 sonnets are addressed to the 'Fair Youth'. The sonnets No. 127 to 154 are directed at the 'Dark Lady'. Before reading the following three poems, find as many reasons as possible to explain why she might be called 'Dark Lady'.

On the left, you can see two paintings by the famous Italian Renaissance painter Sandro Botticelli. Both are supposed to depict the same woman – Simonetta Vespucci, who was said to be the most beautiful woman in Florence. Botticelli's paintings show what was considered to be the ideal woman. Compare these portrayals with Shakespeare's description of his mistress in Sonnet No. 130 and explain the differences you detect.

No. 130

My mistress' eyes are nothing like the sun;
Coral is far more red than her lips' red.
If snow be white, why then her breasts are dun;
If hairs be wires, black wires grow on her head.
I have seen roses damasked, red and white,
But no such roses see I in her cheeks;
And in some perfumes is there more delight
Than in the breath that from my mistress reeks.
I love to hear her speak, yet well I know
That music hath a far more pleasing sound.
I grant I never saw a goddess go:
My mistress, when she walks, treads on the ground.
  And yet, by heaven, I think my love as rare
  As any she belied with false compare.

reeks is emitted
treads on ground walks on the ground
belied lied about
compare comparison

No. 127

In the old age black was not counted fair,
Or if it were, it bore not beauty's name;
But now is black beauty's successive heir,
And beauty slandered with bastard shame:
For since each hand hath put on nature's power,
Fairing the foul with art's false borrowed face,
Sweet beauty hath no name, no holy bower,
But is profaned, if not lives in disgrace.
Therefore my mistress' eyes are raven black,
Her brow so suited, and they mourners seem
At such who, not born fair, no beauty lack,
Sland'ring creation with a false esteem.
Yet so they mourn, becoming of their woe,
That every tongue says beauty should look so.

In the old age In the past
counted considered to be
fair has a double meaning; here it means first and foremost 'beautiful', but also carries the meaning of 'light'
is black beauty's successive heir black is the heir to the title of beauty
since since the moment
Fairing making beautiful
the foul ugliness
bower shrine
But is ... disgrace beauty is either cast out of the temple or disgraced
so suited being the same
becoming of ideally suited to
woe grief

No. 131

Thou art as tyrannous, so as thou art,
As those whose beauties proudly make them cruel;
For well thou know'st to my dear doting heart
Thou art the fairest and most precious jewel.
Yet, in good faith, some say that thee behold,
Thy face hath not the power to make love groan.
To say they err I dare not to be bold,
Although I swear it to myself alone.
And, to be sure that is not false I swear,
A thousand groans, but thinking on thy face,
One on another's neck, do witness bear
Thy black is fairest in my Judgement's place.
In nothing art thou black save in thy deeds,
And thence this slander, as I think, proceeds.

doting infatuated, in love
to behold to catch sight of
groan sigh
Thy black ... place I chose your blackness over everything else
slander defamatory statements

Activities

Characterising the 'Dark Lady'

1. After having read the three sonnets, go over your lists and decide which of your ideas apply to Shakespeare's 'Dark Lady'. Quote evidence from the text.
2. Reread the sonnets and decide if anything needs to be added.
3. Imagine the 'Dark Lady' was an acquaintance of yours and describe her to a friend. You may decide if you want to see her the same way the speaker does or if you want to see her more critically.

Triangular Relationships – The Fair Youth – the Dark Lady – the Poet: Sonnets No. 40 and No. 144

Two men – one woman: What kind of situation might occur? Write a brief story before reading Shakespeare's sonnets No. 40 and No. 144.

No. 40

Take all my loves, my love, yea, take them all;
What hast thou then more than thou hadst before?
No love, my love, that thou mayst true love call;
All mine was thine before thou hadst this more.
Then, if for my love thou my love receivest,
I cannot blame thee for my love thou usest;
But yet be blamed, if thou this self deceivest
By wilful taste of what thyself refusest.
I do forgive thy robbery, gentle thief,
Although thou steal thee all my poverty;
And yet, love knows, it is a greater grief
To bear love's wrong than hate's known injury.
Lascivious grace, in whom all ill well shows;
Kill me with spites; yet we must not be foes.

spites nastiness

No. 144

Two loves I have, of comfort and despair,
Which like two spirits do suggest me still.
The better angel is a man right fair,
The worser spirit a woman coloured ill.
To win me soon to hell my female evil
Tempteth my better angel from my side,
And would corrupt my saint to be a devil,
Wooing his purity with her foul pride;
And whether that my angel be turned fiend
Suspect I may, yet not directly tell;
But being both from me, both to each friend,
I guess one angel in another's hell.
Yet this shall ne'er know, but live in doubt
Till my bad angel fire my good one out.

suggest me still tempt or lure me all the time

Tempteth Tempts

fiend enemy

both ... friend The Dark Lady and the Fair Youth are away from the poet and both are friends.

◀ The word 'hell' refers to three different aspects simultaneously: 1. to a situation between man and woman that has become dangerously close to a physical relationship, 2. the confusion of passion, 3. a vagina

Activities

The triangular relationship

1. Read sonnets No. 40 and No. 144 and decide which of the following sentences most accurately summarizes the situation between the Dark Lady, the Fair Youth and the Poet:
   a) The Poet is jealous because the Dark Lady has left him for the Fair Youth.
   b) The Fair Youth and the Dark Lady are married, but the Dark Lady is betraying her husband with the Poet.
   c) The Poet is uneasy and perhaps even jealous because he is uncertain whether the Fair Youth is betraying him with the Dark Lady.
   d) The Dark Lady is a prostitute who has sexual intercourse with both, the Poet and the Fair Youth.
   e) Both the Poet and the Fair Youth have proposed to the Dark Lady, who cannot make up her mind which offer she wants to accept.
   f) The Poet is afraid of the Fair Youth's revenge because he has eloped with his mistress.
2. Briefly compare sonnets No. 40 and No. 144 with respect to the sentiments the Poet expresses.

Analysing poetry once more

3. Find at least five different stylistic devices employed in Sonnet No. 40 and explain the effect they have.

4. Sonnet No. 144 is full of opposites. Complete the table:

love of comfort (l. 1)	love of despair (l. 1)

Shakespeare's poetry is famous for its **imagery**, i.e. the usage of metaphors and similes. Often imagery taken from one particular field of metaphor contributes to the specific tone of a poem or play.

nurseth feeds

Desperate Love – Sonnet No. 147

No. 147

My love is as a ______, longing still
For that which longer nurseth the ______,
Feeding on that which doth preserve the ______,
Th'uncertain ______ appetite to please.
My reason, the ______ to my love,
Angry that his ______ are not kept,
Hath left me, and I desperate now approve
Desire is death, which ______ did except.
Past ______ I am, now reason is past ______,
And frantic- ______ with evermore ______;
My thoughts and my discourse as ______ 's are,
At random from the truth vainly ______;
For I have sworn thee ______ and thought thee ______,
Who art as ______ as ______ , as ______ as ______.

Activities

1. Some words have been cut out of this sonnet. Take the words from the box below to fill the gaps. (Tip: Metre and rhyme might help you.)

black	madmen	mad	bright	
physician	night	disease	cure	
prescriptions	sickly (= sick)	dark		
fever	ill	physic (= physician)		
express'd	care	unrest	hell	fair

2. Which word fields are the words taken from?
3. In which way does the usage of imagery help to structure the poem?

The Dark Lady – Jigsaw Pieces Only

It is already difficult to say who the Fair Youth might have been, but this is nothing compared to the difficulties that are attached to saying anything certain about the unknown mistress that the sonnets No. 127 to 154 are addressed to. In the sonnets she is described as cruel and promiscuous. People do not seem to think well of her (Sonnet No. 133). The speaker sometimes mocks her dark looks (Sonnet No. 130) and sometimes talks about her 'pretty looks' (Sonnet No. 139). Although her character is depicted as flawed, one can at least say in her favour that she appears to have been an excellent musician (Sonnet No. 128).

Some literary experts claim that she is purely fictional, and for this reason, do not deem it necessary to find out if there ever was a historical 'Dark Lady'. Others believe, however, that she, like the Fair Youth, was a historical person and have thus tried to find out who she might have been. As the 'Dark Lady' might have had a relationship with the 'Fair Youth', her identity partly depends on the answer to the question of who Mr W. H. was and whether or not he is also the 'Fair Youth'. Because this question cannot be answered with any great certainty, the question of who the 'Dark Lady' might have been is even more difficult to answer. Nevertheless, several candidates have been suggested:

- Mary Fitton, maid of honour to Queen Elizabeth I and William Herbert's mistress
- Elizabeth Vernon, lady-in-waiting to Queen Elizabeth I and later Henry Wriothesley's wife
- Emilia Bassano, the wife of Alfonso Lanier and daughter of the Italian musician Baptist Bassano
- Mistress Davenant, the wife of John Davenant, and the host of the Inn of the Golden Cross, where Shakespeare used to stay on his way from London to Stratford-upon-Avon
- Lucy Negro of Clerkenwell, a well-known prostitute of African origin

Mary Fitton

Elizabeth Vernon

Activities

1. For each candidate, find at least one reason why she might have been suggested.
2. Look for further information.
   a) Search the Internet to get more pieces of information on one of the five women.
   b) List the facts that suggest that your candidate is in fact the 'Dark Lady' and those that make it seem doubtful.
   c) Present your results in class.

'Star-Crossed Lovers ...' – Epilogue

Sonnets Hidden in Shakespeare's Play 'Romeo and Juliet'

Although Shakespeare is well-known as the author of a large number of poems, he is even more famous as a playwright. One of his most famous tragedies, 'Romeo and Juliet', was written at approximately the same time as the sonnets. This might be the reason why certain aspects of the play bear some resemblance to the sonnets. First and foremost, it deals with the same topic – love. In addition, various sonnets are hidden in the play. Below you will find the prologue of the play and an excerpt from the fifth scene of the first act.

The Prologue

[Enter Chorus]

CHORUS Two households, both alike in dignity,
In fair Verona, where we lay our scene,
From ancient grudge break to new mutiny,
Where civil blood makes civil hands unclean.
From forth the fatal loins of these two foes
A pair of star-crossed lovers take their life;
Whose misadventured piteous overthrows
Doth with their death bury their parents' strife.
The fearful passage of their death-marked love,
And the continuance of their parents' rage,
Which, but their children's end, naught could remove,
Is now the two hours' traffic of our stage
The which if you with patient ears attend;
What here shall miss, our toil shall strive to mend.

[Exit.]

traffic of our stage performance

Because of its shape, Shakespeare's theatre was called 'The Globe'.

Activity

In the prologue, the most important events of the play 'Romeo and Juliet' are summarized.

Getting to know the play

1. Read it, and explain in modern English what this tragedy is about.
2. Having an actor speak the prologue before the actual play begins means the audience already knows how the love story they are going to see will end. Why might they still be interested in viewing the play?

The following scene describes the first meeting of the 'star-crossed' lovers at a masked ball at the Capulets', Juliet's parents. Romeo and his friends are not invited, but go there in disguise. Upon seeing each other, Romeo and Juliet instantly fall in love with one another. What you see below are the first words the two ever speak to each other.

Act I, Scene 5, 95 – 120

ROMEO If I profane with my unworthiest hand
This holy shrine, the gentle sin is this;
My lips, two blushing pilgrims, ready stand
To smooth that rough touch with a tender kiss.
JULIET Good pilgrim, you do wrong your hand too much,
Which mannerly devotion shows in this;
For saints have hands that pilgrims' hands do touch,
And palm to palm is holy palmers' kiss.
ROMEO Have not saints lips, and holy palmers too?
JULIET Ay pilgrim, lips that they must use in prayer.
ROMEO O, then, dear saint, let lips do what hands do!
They pray; grant thou, lest faith turn in despair.
JULIET Saints do not move, though grant for prayers' sake.
ROMEO Then move not while my prayer's effect I take.
Thus from my lips, by thine my sin is purged. [Kisses her.]

pilgrim sb who travels for religious reasons

to purge to purify, cleanse

From Baz Luhrmann's film (1996)

From Baz Luhrmann's film (1996)

trespass sin, **to trespass** to enter sb else's territory without permission

chinks money

JULIET Then have my lips the sin that they have took.
ROMEO Sin from thy lips? O trespass sweetly urged!
Give me my sin again. [Kisses her.]
JULIET You kiss by th' book.
NURSE Madam, your mother craves a word with you.
ROMEO What is her mother?
NURSE Marry, bachelor,
Her mother is the lady of the house,
And a good lady, and a wise and virtuous.
I nursed her daughter that you talked withal.
I tell you, he that can have hold of her
Shall have the chinks.
ROMEO Is she a Capulet?
O dear account! My life is my foe's debt.

Activities

The hidden sonnet

1. a) Find the sonnet in this excerpt from the play.
   b) How does the fact that some of the words that Romeo and Juliet say to each other are written in the form of sonnet help to emphasize the meaning of their words?

The play in performance

2. View Baz Luzman's version of this scene and explain Juliet's clothing with reference to the text.

The Sonnets Revised

Activities

Getting the basics right

1. Now that you have become familiar with Shakespeare's sonnets, you have probably realized that they form a cycle. One might even claim that they tell a love story. Briefly summarize that story.

Making a movie

2. In order to teach young people more about Shakespeare, a movie about the sonnets is being planned.
   a) Search the Internet to find pictures of actors who you would like to play the Poet, the Fair Youth and the Dark Lady. Explain your choices.
   b) Write the script for one scene of the movie. If possible, include quotations from one or several sonnets.
   c) Act out your scene in class or film it at home and present it in class.

Glossary

Expression	Explanation	Example
Alliteration	Alliteration is when several succeeding words begin with the same letter.	'And every fair from fair sometime declines' (18, l. 7)
Anaphora	Anaphora is when the same word is repeated at the beginning of succeeding sentences.	'So long as men can breathe, or eyes can see, So long lives this, and this gives life to thee.' (18, ll. 13/14)
Antithesis	Antihesis is a rhetorical device in which opposites are directly contrasted with each other.	'In old age black was not counted fair' (127, l. 1)
Chiasmus	In this figure of speech, the structures of two clauses are inverted.	'So long lives this and this gives life to thee.' (18, l. 14)
Couplet	A couplet is a pair of rhyming lines.	'But were some child of yours alive that time, You should live twice, in it and in my rhyme.' (17, ll. 13/14)
Iambic pentameter	Iambic pentameter is the type of verse which Shakespeare uses most often. Some people believe that it evokes a sound that is similar to the beat of the human heart.	'The better angel is a man right fair' x x́ x x́ x x́ x x́ x x́ (144, l. 3)
Imagery	Images are used to illustrate abstract ideas and to evoke vivid mental pictures. Metaphors and similes are both different types of imagery.	'And beauty slander'd with a bastard shame' (127, l. 4)
Metaphor	The term metaphor refers to a direct comparison between two seemingly unrelated things.	'Let me not to the marriage of true minds' (116, l. 1)
Oxymoron	An oxymoron is the combination of two opposites.	'master-mistress' (20, l. 2)
Parallelism	The term parallelism is used to refer to sentences in which corresponding elements use the same grammatical structures.	'The better angel is a man right fair, The worser spirit a woman colour'd ill.' (144, ll. 3/4)
Personification	In personification, objects or abstract things are attributed human qualities.	'The age to come would say ...' (17, l. 7)
Pun	A pun is a play on words using different meanings of the same word.	'So thou, being rich in Will, add to thy Will On will of mine, to make thy large Will more.' (135, ll. 11/12) ('Will' has a triple meaning: 1) It's Shakespeare's and his supposed lover's first name, 2) it can mean 'volition', and 3) it is used to refer to male and female sexual organs.)

Expression	Explanation	Example
Quatrain	The term quatrain refers to four lines belonging together.	'Shall I compare thee to a summer's day? / Thou art more lovely and more temperate: / Rough winds do shake the darling buds of May, / And summer's lease hath all too short a date.' (18, ll. 1–4)
Repetition	This rhetoric device involves using the same word twice or more often in order to stress its meaning.	'No love, my love, that thou mayst true love call' (40, l. 3)
Rhetorical question	A question to which the answer is obvious is called a rhetorical question.	'Shall I compare thee to a summer's day?' (18, l. 1)
Rhyme	A rhyme means matching sounds at the end of two or more lines.	'But were some child of yours alive that time, / You should live twice, in it and in my rhyme.' (17, ll. 13/14)
Simile	A simile is a comparison between two seemingly unrelated things in which the words 'as' or 'like' are used.	'How like a winter hath my absence been' (97, l. 1)

Acknowledgements

Texts

Tom Schulman: *Dead Poets Society: The Screenplay*. Harvest Moon Publishing, Santa Monica 2000

Peter Hyland: *An Introduction to Shakespeare. The Dramatist in his Context*, Macmillan, London 1996, pp. 39–40

Russ McDonald: 'Early Modern English', from: Russ McDonald (ed.): The Bedford Companion to Shakespeare, Palgrave, New York 1996, pp. 182–184

Oscar Wilde: *The Portrait of Mr W. H.*, Hesperus Press, London 2003

Illustrations

Royal Shakespeare Theatre Collection, Stratford-upon-Avon: p. 5 top; ullstein bild – NTPL: p. 5 centre; © 1989 Touchstone Pictures: p. 6, 7, 8, 9; © Library of the University of California, Los Angeles: p. 10, 26 top; Shakespeare Birthplace Trust, Stratford-upon-Avon: p. 17 top; Peter Apian: Cosmographia, Antwerpen 1524: p. 19; Archiv für Kunst und Geschichte, Berlin: p. 20, 25; ullstein bild - Granger Collection: p. 26 bottom left; © Hesperus Press Ltd.: p. 29; IFA-BILDERTEAM – TPC: p. 32 left; Peter-T. Schulz: p. 32 centre left; Schapowalow/Huber: p. 32 centre right; © die bildstelle/REX FEATURES LTD.: p. 32 right; Bildarchiv Preußischer Kulturbesitz, Berlin: p. 36 left; © Städel Museum, Frankfurt: p. 36 right; © Jonathan Webb: p. 42; © 1997 Twentieth Century Fox Film Corporation: p. 43, 44; other illustrations: Verlagsarchiv Schöningh.

Every effort has been made to supply complete copyright information for the texts and pictures included here. Should such entries be incomplete or contain errors, we request copyright owners to contact the publishers so that we can proceed with the necessary corrections.